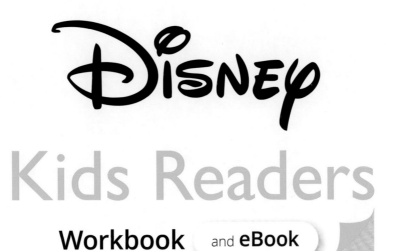

Disney

Kids Readers

Workbook and **eBook**

Level **4**

Sandy Zerva

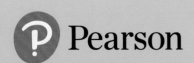

P Pearson

Contents

Book 1

Disney · PIXAR

TOY STORY 3

How do the characters feel?
Think and talk.

Vocabulary

1 **Complete the sentences.**

1 Woody is a s h e r i f f , Jessie is a _____ _____ _____ _____ _____
and Buzz is a _____ _____ _____ _____ _____ _____ _____ _____ _____ _____ .

2 Woody flew over the d _____ _____ _____ _____ _____ _____ e _____ _____ _____ _____
on a _____ _____ _____ _____ .

2 **Sort the words.**

throw away
chute
_____
_____

prison   ~~chute~~

trash

roof   sheriff

dumpster

attic

basket   box

college

classroom

for students
_____
_____

parts of a house
_____
_____

thieves don't
like them
_____
_____

keep things in them
_____
_____

3 **Put the words in alphabetical order.**

trash   switch   ~~attic~~   roof   box

1 attic   **2** _____   **3** _____   **4** _____   **5** _____

Story

1 ▸ **Read and circle.**

1 The toys wanted to go to Sunnyside because
   a they were angry with Woody.
   b it was a new life for them.

2 Buzz put Andy's other toys in prison because
   a he didn't know they were his friends.
   b they weren't nice to him.

3 Woody wrote Bonnie's address on the box because
   a he didn't want to go to college with Andy.
   b he wanted a new, happy life for his friends.

2 ▸ **Compare the scenes.**

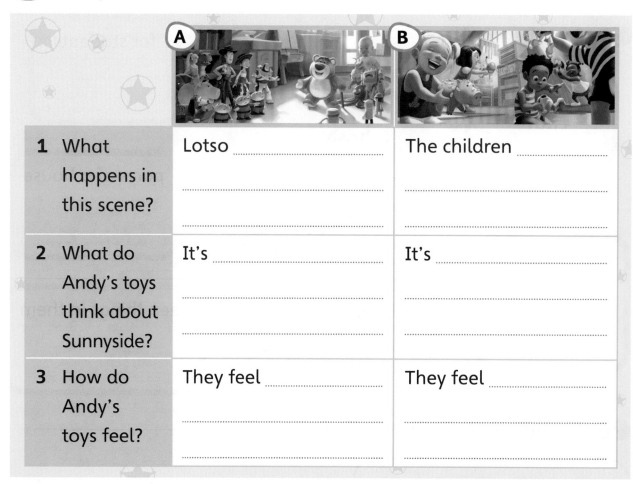

	A	**B**
1 What happens in this scene?	Lotso	The children
2 What do Andy's toys think about Sunnyside?	It's	It's
3 How do Andy's toys feel?	They feel	They feel

3 ▸ **Do you like how the story ends?**

I like/don't like the ending because

Language

1 🎧 **Listen and read.**

💬 Language

What **are** you **going to do** tonight?   I**'m going to play** computer games.

Are you **going to do** your homework?   No, I**'m not**.

Use *be* + *going to* + **verb** to show intention.

2 **Complete the dialogs.**

Gil: What ...are... you .... **do**
         on the weekend?

Anna: I .... to the mall.   **go**

Gil: .... you ....   **buy**
         some new jeans?

Anna: No, I .... I ....   **get**
         a new coat.

3 **Practice in pairs. Talk about your plans for the weekend.**

What are you going to do on Saturday?

I'm going to do the grocery shopping with my parents. In the afternoon, I'm going to visit my cousins.

Who is busier this weekend?

Me   My friend

Phonics

1 🎧 **Listen and check the word you hear.**

1 ⭕ most ⭕ must   **4** ⭕ so ⭕ son

2 ⭕ hop ⭕ hope   **5** ⭕ clock ⭕ close

3 ⭕ love ⭕ low   **6** ⭕ show ⭕ shop

2 🎧 **Write o, o_e, or ow. Then listen and say.**

Mom dr____v____ us here in a box in her car,

To Sunnyside Center. It wasn't s____ hard.

Lots____ the bear said hell____ to us first.

We didn't kn____ it then, but Lots____'s the worst!

____nly Woody knew, and he wanted to g____,

S____ he jumped through the wind____ to the yard bel____.

3 🎧 **Listen and write the words. Then check the words with a long o sound as in *hello*.**

⭕ ph____ ____ ____   ⭕ gl____ ____ ____ ____   ⭕ sn____ ____

⭕ pi____ ____ ____   ⭕ rain____ ____ ____   ⭕ s____ ____ ____ ____

Values: Positivity

1 How do you know these characters think positively? Write.

1 [4] Jesssie says: ....

2 [18] Andy says: ....

3 [20] Buzz says: ....

2 How do you stay positive about changes in your life? Check (✔). Then add one more.

- ◯ I try to find the good things about it.
- ◯ I don't hide my feelings. I talk with my friends and family.
- ◯ I think of ways to make things better.
- ◯ Sometimes there is nothing I can do and that's okay.
- ◯ ....

3 Share.

> When I'm worried about a change, I try to find the good things about it.

4 💡 Read and then role play. Help Sally think positively.

Sally and her family are going to move to a new town.

> I love my house! My new room isn't going to be the same!

> I don't want to change schools. I'm not going to have friends there!

> I don't want to leave my friends!

Find Out

1 What do the numbers refer to? Write notes.

4   The number of ....

....

24   The number of ....

....

40,000 The number of ....

....

1995   The ....

....

2 How were the first animated movies different than the movies they make now?

Writing tip

The last Toy Story movie was in 2019.
In 1995, it was the first time to make a movie in this way.

When you start a sentence with a time reference, add a comma.

3 Write. Add commas where necessary.

1 The first *Toy Story* movie came out **1995**

2 The second movie, *Toy Story 2*, came out **1999**

3 .... they made *Toy Story 3*.   **2010**

4 The first *Toy Story* special for TV, *Toy Story of Terror*,   **2013**
was ....

5 .... there was another *Toy Story* Special: **2014**
Toy Story that Time Forgot.

Game   Follow the Path

Start

1 Why does Andy put his toys in a bag?

2 Choose the odd one out.

dumpster
trash
prison
chute

3 How did the filmmakers make the first Toy Story movie? Put the stages in order.

complete movie
computer models
sketches

7 Did the toys like the daycare center? Why/Why not?

6 What are you going to do on the weekend? Say two sentences.

5 You are 19 years old. Where can you go to study?

4 How did Woody leave the daycare center?

8 You're in prison! Lose a turn.

9 Spell the words. Is the final sound the same?

rainb..........
sn..........
pian..........

10 Who says that? Do you agree?

"Children don't really love their toys!"

11 Make a sentence about the picture.

Finish

14 Spell it.

This is a y ....
p h ....

13 Why is Andy taking the box to this house?

12 True or False?

Andy's toys are sad after Andy drives to college. They're going to have an unhappy life with Bonnie.

Now I can...

◯ understand what happens and why in a story about toys.

◯ ask and say what people are going to do.

◯ read, spell, and say words with o, o_e, and ow.

What does this picture tell
you about Moana?
Think and talk.

Vocabulary

1 Read the clues 1–5 and write the words. There is one extra.

attack   heart   treasure   hook   pretend   reef

1 It's an actor's job to do this. ....

2 You're a fish and you don't like this! ....

3 Pirates do this—be careful! ....

4 It's under the sea—it's beautiful! ....

5 You cannot live without this. ....

2 Match the opposites. Then choose and write.

1 darkness   **2** fix   **3** treasure   **4** large   **5** pull

a little   **b** push   **c** break   **d** light   **e** trash

They're .... the boat out of the water.

He's .... the boat into the water.

3 Cross out the extra letters. Write them in the boxes. Unscramble them to find the secret word.

1 island (e)   **3** houok ( )   **5** rorck ( )   **7** reefe ( )

2 pirrates ( )   **4** atttack ( )   **6** cavae ( )   **8** pussh ( )

The secret word is: ☐ ☐ ☐ ☐ ☐ ☐ ☐ ☐

Story

1 Write. Use one word for each gap.

1 Little Moana found a green _____ in the ocean.

2 Moana didn't listen to her _____ and left the island to find Te Fiti.

3 In _____ _____, Maui and Moana found Maui's hook.

4 Maui's hook helped him change into different _____.

5 Maui fought Te Kā and she broke his _____.

6 Moana knew that _____ _____ and Te Fiti were the same.

2 Write about Moana. Find examples in the story.

Moana is not afraid.

She leaves her island.

_____

_____

Moana is smart.

_____

_____

_____

3 In the story, Maui changes into different animals. Imagine you have the same power. Which animal do you become? Why?

I become a _____

because _____

_____

Language

1 **Listen and read.**

> ### 💬 Language
> Storms **can** be dangerous. You **could** get hurt.
>
> Use **can** to talk about things that are possible and certain.
>
> Use **could** to talk about things that are possible, but not certain.

2 **Write. Use *can* or *could*.**

1 In winter, the waves on this beach .... get really big.

2 We .... swim to the island. It's possible, I think.

3 That thing in the sky .... be a bird. I'm not sure.

4 You .... catch lots of fish here. It's the best place for fishing.

5 I don't want to go into the cave. It .... be dangerous.

3 **You want to go hiking. In pairs, talk about why you want to take these things with you.**

raincoat

map

bug spray

water bottle

sunscreen

flashlight

cap

snack

Let's take our raincoats.

You're right.
It could rain.

Phonics

1 🎧 **Listen and circle the words with a long u sound as in *moon*.**

1 new   not   noon   **4** room   run   brush

2 cool   foot   food   **5** tissue   threw   truck

3 glue   glove   grew   **6** stew   school   study

2 🎧 **Write ew, oo, or ue. Then listen and say.**

Maui fl............,   Moana kn............

And the sky was bl.............   That the heart was tr.............

No stars, no m............n.   She could go home s............n.

3 🎧 **Do the crossword. Spell words with ew, oo, or ue. Find the secret word. Listen and check.**

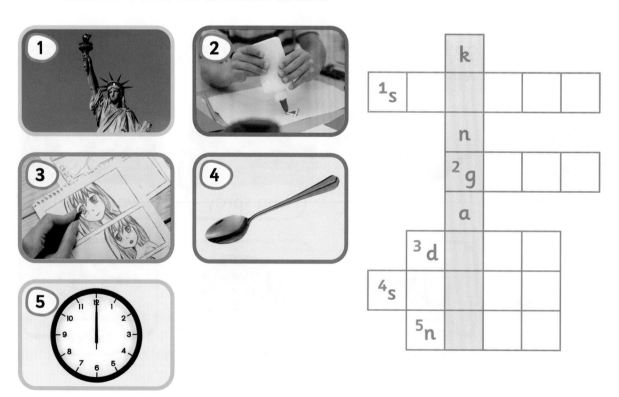

The secret word is: ☐ ☐ ☐ ☐ ☐ ☐ ☐ ☐

Values: Respect

1 **Match 1–3 to a–c.**

1 Gramma wants Moana to ......

2 The pictures on the cave walls ......

3 The pictures help Moana to ......

a tell the story of the people of Motunui.

b understand who she is and what she must do.

c learn about her family's past.

2 **Make a wall painting about your family. Draw members of your family wearing or holding things that show who they are or were.**

3 **Share.**

This is my grandad, Leo. He has a guitar because he loves playing music. He's wearing his pilot's hat because he was a pilot.

4 **Read and talk. What are the ways you could record your family history?**

Family history is important. We can learn a lot from what happened in the past. When we don't record it, we can forget it. What can we do so we don't forget the past?

Find Out

1 **Read and check True or False.**

		True	False
1	Hawaii is an American State.	◯	◯
2	Hawaii is a big island.	◯	◯
3	The last volcano to erupt was 8 million years ago.	◯	◯
4	The size of the land in Hawaii changes all the time.	◯	◯

2 **Some people like to get close to volcanoes. Is it safe?**

Writing tip

Volcanic eruptions can be small or very big.

> Use *or* to link choices or possibilities.

3 **Write. Use *or* to join the sentences.**

1 Lava can be very thin. Lava can be very thick.
Lava can be very thin or very thick.

2 Hot lava can be bright orange. Hot lava can be bright red.

....

3 Do volcanoes make noise? Do volcanoes erupt quietly?

....

4 Volcanoes can grow in thousands of years. Volcanoes can grow in a few days.

....

Kilauea, Hawaii.

Game Spin the Wheel

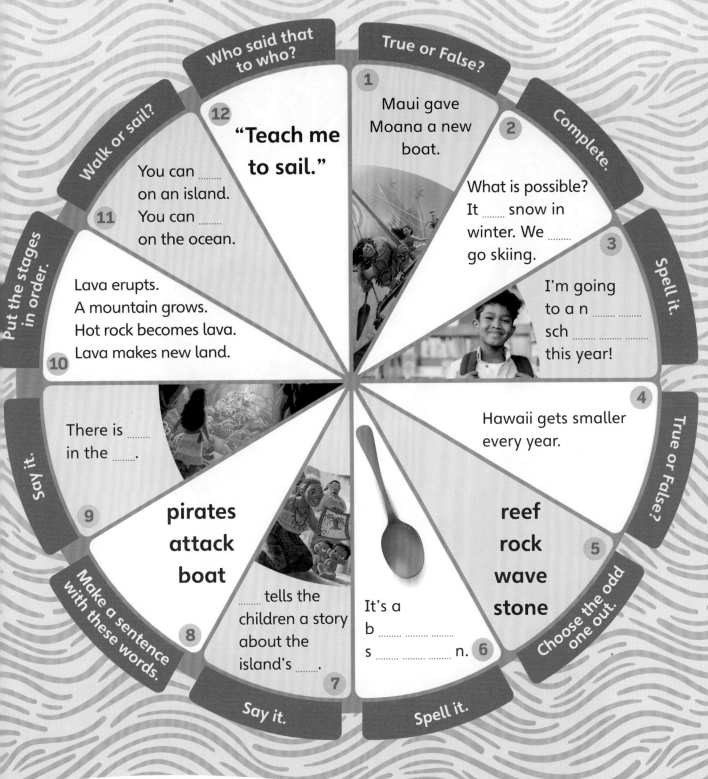

Who said that to who?

12 "Teach me to sail."

True or False?

1 Maui gave Moana a new boat.

Complete.

2 What is possible? It .... snow in winter. We .... go skiing.

Walk or sail?

You can .... on an island. You can .... on the ocean.

11

Spell it.

3 I'm going to a n .... sch .... this year!

Put the stages in order.

Lava erupts.
A mountain grows.
Hot rock becomes lava.
Lava makes new land.

10

True or False?

4 Hawaii gets smaller every year.

Say it.

There is .... in the ....

9

Make a sentence with these words.

pirates
attack
boat

8

Say it.

.... tells the children a story about the island's ....

7

Spell it.

It's a
b ....
s .... n. 6

Choose the odd one out.

reef
rock
wave
stone

5

Now I can...

○ understand what happens and why in a story about sailing.

○ talk about things that are possible using *can* and *could*.

○ read, spell, and say words with ew, oo, and ue.

{}

Book 3

THE LION KING

What are the characters
looking at? Think and talk.

Vocabulary

1 **Circle the odd one out.**

1 bone   deep   paw   tail   **3** desert   jungle   stampede   valley

2 safe   dead   kill   die   **4** voice   sound   ground   noise

2 **Label the pictures.**

lion   ....

3 **Do the crossword.**

safe   dead   desert   secret   stampede   paw   valley   bones

1 The jungle is not a .... place for people.

2 A lion's foot is called its ....

3 The land between two mountains is a ....

4 It doesn't often rain in the ....

5 A lot of animals running fast is a ....

6 After the stampede, Mufasa was ....

7 Don't tell them! It's a ....

8 Inside your leg there are three big ....

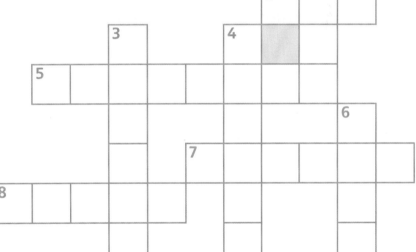

Story

1 **Which sentences are main ideas in the story? Which one isn't? Check (✔) or cross (✗).**

1 ◯ Do not believe all the things people tell you.

2 ◯ You can't change the past, but you can learn from it.

3 ◯ You can't be friends with people who are different than you.

2 **Put the events in the correct order in the story arc.**

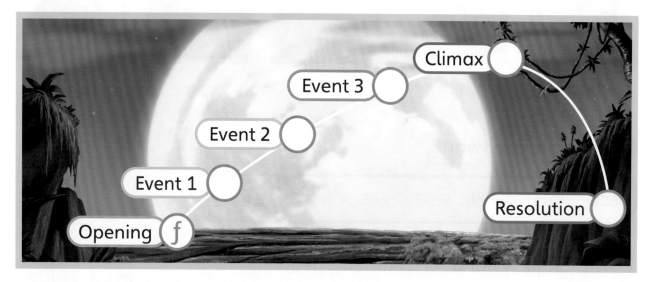

a Simba meets Timon and Pumbaa. He grows up away from home.

b Simba fights Scar. He wins. Scar leaves.

c Scar kills Mufasa. Simba believes he killed him and runs away.

d Simba and Nala meet again. She asks him to go back.

e Simba becomes king. He remembers his father's words.

f Mufasa teaches Simba how to become a good king.

3 **Circle what you think and explain why.**

1 Young Simba thinks, "I killed my father!" and runs away.
He did the **right** / **wrong** thing. ....

2 Adult Simba fights Scar and wins. He tells Scar to run away and never come back.
He did the **right** / **wrong** thing. ....

Language

1 🎧 **Listen and read.**

2 **Write. Put the verbs in the past simple tense. Are they talking about a safari, or a TV show?**

1 Alice: The hungry lioness ____saw____ (see) the baby elephant and _____ (go) near it.

Brent: _____ she _____ (catch) it?

Alice: No, she _____ . Its mom _____ (come) and the lioness _____ (run) away.

2 Chris: The wildebeest _____ (find) a river. They _____ (drink) water and _____ (eat) some grass.

Dot: _____ you _____ (take) any photos?

Chris: Yes, I _____ . Here they are.

3 **Play a game. Choose verbs from the box. Use each verb only once for a question and answer.**

bring catch come draw drink eat feel
go hide run say see sleep take think

I went on safari.

Yes, I did. I took some photos.

Did you see any lions?

Where did you sleep?

Phonics

1 🎧 Listen and match words with a long i sound as in *hide*.

1 pretty   why   city   cry   **3** drive   nice   bring   ship

2 high   wind happy dry   **4** give   tie   write   bridge

2 🎧 Write **ie**, **i_e**, **igh**, or **y**. Then listen and say.

Simba looked up at the stars and cr＿＿＿d, "Wh＿＿＿?"

Mufasa sm＿＿＿l＿＿＿d down at his son from the sk＿＿＿.

The sun's l＿＿＿t arr＿＿＿v＿＿＿d at the end of the n＿＿＿t,

And the true Lion King was ready to f＿＿＿t.

3 🎧 Do the crossword. Spell words with **ie**, **i_e**, **igh**, or **y**.
Find and draw the secret word. Listen and check.

Values: Honesty

1 **Answer the questions.**

1 Why does Simba lie to his parents?
2 The hyenas find Simba and Nala.
   What could happen?
3 It's wrong to lie. Does Simba
   understand that?

2 **Read some reasons why you mustn't lie. Add one more. Think about what happened one time you lied.**

1 People learn the truth in the end.
2 People don't trust liars.
3 You could hurt people.
4 It's better to tell the truth and learn from your mistakes.
5 ....

3 **Share.**

I wanted to cycle to the river with my friends, but my mom said no. I lied and said I was at my friend's house. My mom found out. She was angry because it was dangerous.

4  **Read and talk. What could Tania do? What could happen?**

Tania went to the movies on Saturday. Her friend Ben went to another movie that his parents didn't want him to see. He asked Tania to lie to his parents for him and say that he was with her. Tania doesn't know what to do.

Find Out

1 Answer the questions. Write notes.

1 What do lions do for most of the day? ....

2 What do male lions do for the group? ....

3 What do lionesses do for the group? ....

4 Why is playtime important for lion cubs? ....

2  Why do lions sleep so much / hunt in groups / roar?

Writing tip

Lions sleep for about 20 hours every day.
A lioness has between two and six cubs.

Use *about* to say a little more or less than a number or amount.
Use *between ... and ...* with two numbers.

3 Write. Use *about* or *between*.

1 A lion's body is .... long. 184–208 cm

2 Adult lions can eat .... of meat in
one meal. 40 kg

3 Lions begin to grow old when they are

.... years old. 10–15

4 Male lions are .... heavier than lionesses. 60 kg

5 Baby cubs are .... 1.2–2.1 kg

6 They start walking at .... old. three weeks

Game Connect Four in a Line

1 Why did Simba go to the dangerous place?

He was excited and wanted to see it.

Scar told him to go there.

2

What can you see? Say two sentences.

3 Complete.

Lions   Lionesses

.... protect the group from other animals.

.... hunt for food.

4 Say it.

Don't tell them. It's a ....!

5

There are elephant .... there.

6 Which word sounds different?

dry   pie   happy

fight   sit   white

7 Say it.

Simba ran away. He was scared and .... He was hungry, and ...., and ....

8 Make two sentences about the past.

fight   hide   go   eat

9 Join the opposites.

safe   desert

dead   in danger

jungle   alive

10 Say it. Use the past tense.

see   hear

Simba .... his father in the sky. He .... his voice.

11 Say it.

Simba .... to his father. He was ....

12 Name all the kings of the Pride Lands in the story in the correct order.

13 Spell it.

I see a w .... bird in the s .... It can f ....!

14 Who says that?

"I live inside you, Simba."

15 Put the animals in order from smallest to biggest.

lion   meerkat

lioness   warthog

16

What was Scar's secret?

Now I can...

○ understand what happens and why in a story about lions.

○ talk about doing things in the past using the past simple.

○ read, spell, and say words with ie, i_e, igh, and y.

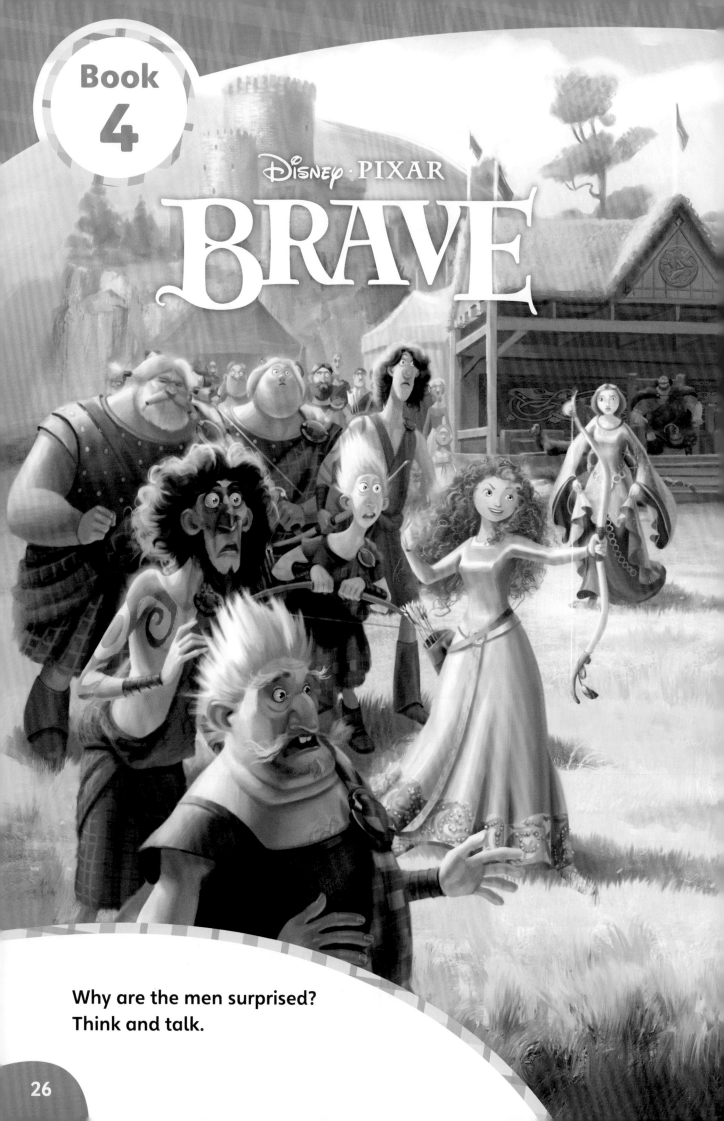

Book 4

Disney · PIXAR

BRAVE

Why are the men surprised?
Think and talk.

Vocabulary

1 Find and circle the words. Use the extra letters to find the secret message.

1 yobraveu
2 mapartust

3 mechoosend
4 whmarryat

5 yoperfectu
6 brofreeke

Message: ....

2 Match the word in the picture with a or b. Make a sentence with the two words.

1 stone
(a) hard
b soft

2 archery
a ball
b sports

3 fight
a scarf
b sword

4 witch
a spell
b future

5 mend
a fix
b buy

6 win
a competition
b kingdom

 A stone is hard.

3 Put the words in alphabetical order.

kingdom   witch   sword   free   archery   mend   future   apart   marry

1 ....

2 ....

3 ....

4 ....

5 ....

6 ....

7 ....

8 ....

9 ....

Story

1 **Who says this? What are they talking about?**

1

> You must learn how to be a good princess, then I can find you a good husband.

....

....

2

> I'm not going to do what you tell me!

....

....

3

> Long ago, I gave this spell to a prince. It made him stronger than ten men!

....

....

2 **Compare Merida and Elinor. Who do you think changes more?**

	In the beginning	At the end
Elinor	She is .... with Merida's choices. She wants her daughter to	She understands that Merida must decide ....
Merida	She .... with her mother. She doesn't want to	She understands that, as a princess, she must do what is good for .... She wants to ....

3 **Who would / wouldn't you like to be in the story? Why?**

I would / wouldn't like to be .... because ....

28

Language

1 🎧 **Listen and read.**

💬 Language

I **like to play** tennis with my dad. I also **like playing** soccer.

After *like*, *love*, *hate*, *start*, use *to + verb* or **verb + *ing***.

I **want to watch** the game.   I **enjoy listening** to music.

After *want*, *hope*, *learn*, use *to + verb*.

After *enjoy*, *finish*, use **verb + *ing***.

2 **Choose and write. Use the correct form of a verb from the box.**

> see   drive   study   swim   get

1 I hope .... you at my party next Saturday.

2 My sister hates .... up early in the morning.

3 Grandad enjoys .... in the sea in winter.

4 My cousin is learning .... because he's going to buy a car.

5 I finished .... Can I play a video game now?

3 **In pairs, talk about your hobbies. Use verbs from Activity 1, and your own ideas.**

What are your hobbies?

I love writing. I want to write a short story about a witch.

Phonics

1 🎧 **Listen and number.**

( ) bake   ( ) rain   (1) hate   ( ) way   ( ) plane

( ) back   ( ) ran   ( ) hat   ( ) why   ( ) plan

2 🎧 **Write a_e, ai, or ay. Then listen and say.**

Here on a pl____t____

Is a c____k____ I m____d____,

With an interesting t____st____, you s____.

But, w____t—a mist____k____!

You're a bear, I'm afr____d.

We must run aw____ tod____!

3 🎧 **Listen and write the words. Then check the correct picture.**

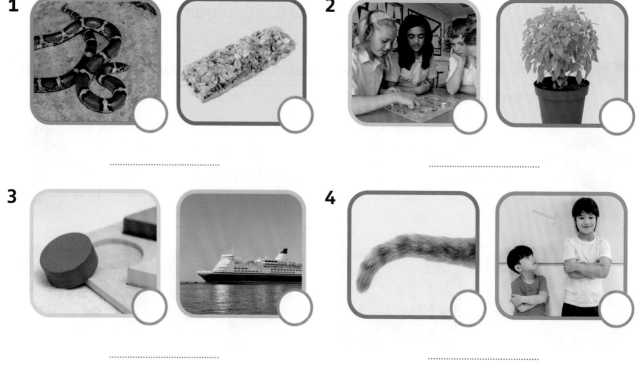

1

2

....

3

4

....

Values: Humility

1 What do we learn from Elinor and Merida's story? Choose a, b, or c.

a Older people learn from younger people.
b Younger people learn from older people.
c All people can learn from other people, at any age.

2 Match the thoughts (1–4) to the advice (a–d). Do you ever think the same things? Check (✔) or cross (✘).

1 ◯ I don't understand this activity. I don't want people to think I'm stupid! ....

2 ◯ I made a mistake, but I'm not going to tell. Smart people don't make mistakes. ....

3 ◯ I don't care what people say. I'm always right! ....

4 ◯ I don't have time to listen to my friend's problems! ....

a You can't be right all the time.
b Always have time for your friends.
c All people make mistakes and learn from them.
d Smart people ask for help.

3 Share.

> Sometimes I don't understand an activity, but I try to ask for help. It's the smart thing to do.

4 Read and talk. What advice could you give Jamie?

Jamie usually gets the best grades in class, and he thinks he is better than his classmates. He never helps them with their work. He often wins the math competitions and the spelling competitions. But he gets angry when he loses. Jamie's classmates don't like him.

Find Out

1   **Read and circle.**

1 The Bayeux tapestry is **the oldest in Europe / about 1,000 years old**.

2 **50,000 people / People of all ages** worked on the Great Tapestry of Scotland.

3 They stitched the tapestry **at work / in their free time**.

4 The Bayeux tapestry is **bigger / smaller** than the Scottish tapestry.

2 **How did people tell stories in the past?**

> *Some **children** worked on the tapestry.*
> *The youngest **child** was four years old.*
>
> Learn the plural spellings for some irregular nouns.

2   **Write the plural form of the words in brackets.**

1 Many .... worked on the Great Tapestry of Scotland. (person)

2 Most .... are very old, but this is new. (tapestry)

3 The tapestry is 469 .... long. (foot)

4 .... and .... stitched their .... into the tapestry. (man, woman, story)

5 Some of the animals it shows are ...., ..., and .... (mouse, sheep, fish)

Game Follow the Path

Start

1 Match the opposites.

mend   brave

afraid   together

apart   break

2 Spell it.

The witch m ___ d ___ a c ___ k ___.

3 What did Merida's mom eat? What happened to her?

4 What does Merida like?

7 Correct the mistakes.

All tapestries are old. People make them with threads of the same color.

6 Spell it.

He's pl ___ ___ ing a computer g ___ m ___.

5 Say it. Use *swim*.

I'm learning ___.
I want ___ in the lake by my house.
I enjoy ___!

8 You got lost in the forest! Lose a turn.

9 Make a sentence with these words.

fight   sword

bear

10 What do you like to do in your free time? Say two sentences.

11 Spell it.

It's r ___ ___ ___ ning tod ___ ___.

Finish

14 Who says this? Who is the prince in this sentence?

"Long ago, I gave this spell to a prince."

13 What is happening?

These men want to ___ Merida. They are ___!

12 True or False?

When Merida mended the tapestry, Elinor changed back into a woman.

Now I can ...

○ understand what happens and why in a story about family and the past.

○ talk about hobbies using *like, love, hate, start, want, hope, learn, enjoy,* and *finish*.

○ read, spell, and say words with a_e, ai, and ay.

What are the characters doing?
Think and talk.

Vocabulary

1 Color the memory balls. Use the colors of the emotions.

 disgusted

 excited

 scared

 mad

 sad

2 Match and write the words with similar meanings.

emotion   fear   core   arrive   unhappy

1 most important ....

2 feeling ....

3 sad ....

4 panic ....

5 appear ....

3 Choose and write. There is one extra word.

together   memory   worried   disgusted   control   saved

1 Grandad's .... is very good.

2 I cannot .... my feelings.

3 A brave woman .... the girl.

4 My sister and I sang a song ....

5 They were .... with the food.

Story

1 **What is the main theme of the story? Check (✔).**

1 You can learn to control your emotions and be happy. Try to hide negative feelings and bad memories. ◯

2 Some emotions are more important than others. Negative emotions like sadness and fear don't help. ◯

3 All emotions are important: you can't have joy without sadness. It is okay to show your emotions. ◯

2 **Answer the questions about this key event in the story.**

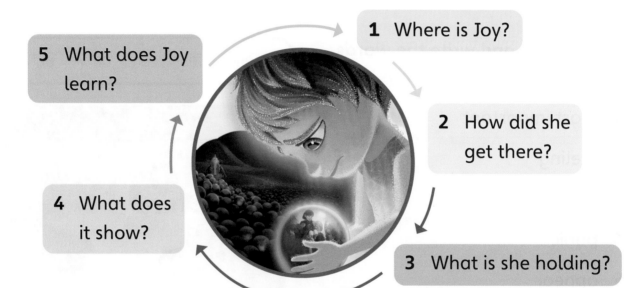

5 What does Joy learn?

1 Where is Joy?

2 How did she get there?

4 What does it show?

3 What is she holding?

3 **Riley's islands of personality are Family, Honesty, Hockey, Friendship and Goofball. What are yours?**

My islands of personality are ....

....

Language

1 **Listen and read.**

> ### 💬 Language
>
> Anna is **the funniest** person in our class.
>
> My dad is **the most helpful** person I know.
>
> That was **the best** memory of the year.
>
> What was **the worst** memory?
>
> Use superlative adjectives to compare more than two things.

2 **Write sentences. Use superlative adjectives.**

1 Today / happy day / of my life!
Today is the happiest day of my life!

2 My sister / good swimmer / in her class.

....

3 Dad / bad dancer / in our family.

....

4 My brother / smart person / I know.

....

5 This / dangerous thing / you can do!

....

3 **In pairs, talk about people you know. Use superlative adjectives.**

> Who's the fastest runner you know?

> My sister. She's the fastest runner in the school.

Phonics

1 🎧 **Listen and check the word you hear.**

1 ⭘ east ⭘ west   **4** ⭘ meet ⭘ met

2 ⭘ leaf ⭘ life   **5** ⭘ cheap ⭘ chip

3 ⭘ feel ⭘ film   **6** ⭘ wheel ⭘ well

2 🎧 **Write ea, ee, or y. Then listen and say.**

Riley's life is happ............

Suddenl............, one w............kend,

She l............ves for a new cit............,

And she can't s............ her friends.

Is she sl............ping or dr............ming?

How does the stor............ end?

3 🎧 **Look and spell words with ea, ee, or y. Listen and check.**

1 ....   **2** ....   **3** ....

4 ....   **5** ....   **6** ....

Values: Sincerity

1 **How does Riley feel before and after talking to her parents?**

Before

After

2 **Circle the answers that are true for you, or add your own answers.**

1 When do you most want to talk about your feelings?

When I feel **sad / happy / worried / afraid / angry / excited /** ....

....

2 Who do you talk to?

My **parents / friends / teacher /** ....

3 What happens after you talk?

I feel that I can make things better. / I understand why I am feeling that way. / ....

3 **Share.**

> When I feel worried, I usually talk to my dad. He always helps me.

4 🔅 **Read and talk. How do you think Bart feels? What can he do?**

Bart and Alex are best friends. Manu is Alex's new friend. Alex and Manu play the same sports and they spend a lot of time together without Bart.

Find Out

1 Check the correct sentences. In pairs, correct the false ones.

1 ◯ The amygdala controls all the emotions you have.

2 ◯ When you are in danger, you must choose quickly what to do.

3 ◯ Panic helps you think quickly.

4 ◯ You can learn how to control your emotions.

2 🔆 Try closing your eyes and breathing deeply. What thing can you think of as you breathe?

📋 **Writing tip**

The girl said, "I feel better now."

Use speech marks to show that a person is speaking.

---

3 Read and add the speech marks.

1 "How are you feeling?" asked Luke's mom.
"I'm worried about the math test today," he said.

2 Please finish your dinner, said Gran.
But I don't like green vegetables, Kim said.
They're disgusting.

3 Petra said, Happy Birthday, Dan! Open your present!
Dan felt happy. This video game is so cool, he said.

4 Max saw the snake first. Don't move! He shouted,
Oh, that was dangerous! cried Ben.

Game Spin the Wheel

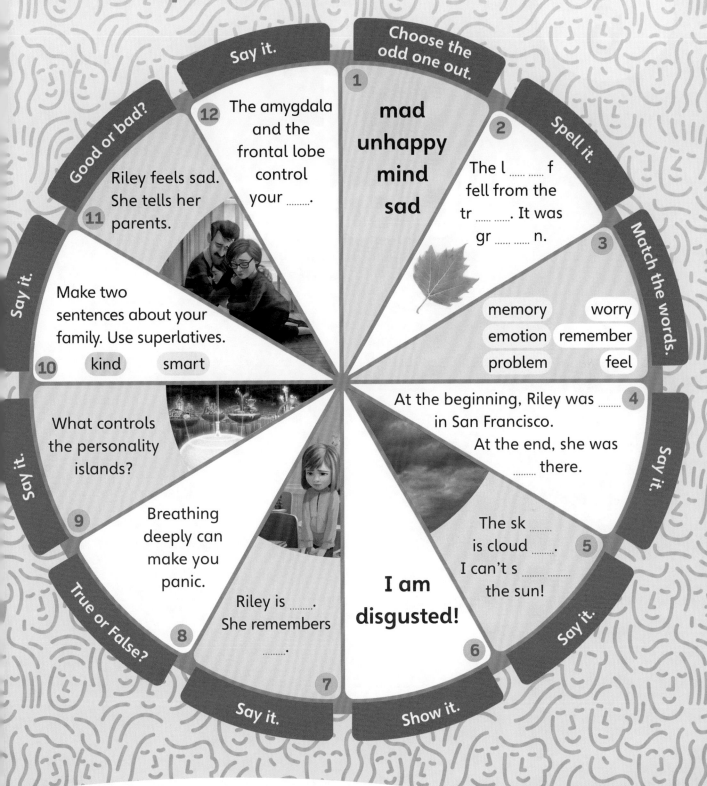

Say it.

12 The amygdala and the frontal lobe control your ....

Choose the odd one out.

1
**mad
unhappy
mind
sad**

Spell it.

2 The l .... f fell from the tr .... It was gr .... n.

Good or bad?

11 Riley feels sad. She tells her parents.

Match the words.

3
memory   worry
emotion   remember
problem   feel

Say it.

Make two sentences about your family. Use superlatives.

10 kind   smart

At the beginning, Riley was .... 4 in San Francisco. At the end, she was .... there.

Say it.

What controls the personality islands?

9

Say it.

Breathing deeply can make you panic.

8 Riley is .... She remembers ....

I am disgusted!

6

The sk .... is cloud .... I can't s .... the sun! 5

Say it.

True or False?

Say it.

7

Show it.

Now I can ...

○ understand what happens and why in a story about changes and emotions.

○ compare people and things using superlative adjectives.

○ read, spell, and say words with ea, ee, and y.

Book 6

Disney · PIXAR

INCREDIBLES 2

Is the train going to go faster or slower? Think and talk.

Vocabulary

1 **Label the pictures. Use verbs from the Glossary.**

1

....

2

....

3

....

4

....

5

....

6

....

2 **Sort the words.** camera   message   helicopter   screen   parachute

Things in the sky ....

Things on a computer ....

3 **Find the words.**

1 It is .... to steal things.

2 Police officers ....
and catch thieves.

3 It is .... to jump out
of a plane with a parachute.

4 You take a photograph with
a ....

5 They nearly died in a car
....

C	A	M	E	R	A	W	O
R	M	Q	D	O	S	G	V
A	C	T	N	O	L	O	R
S	U	C	H	A	S	E	J
H	I	L	L	E	G	A	L
L	L	I	C	V	E	U	Y
V	Q	U	Y	V	V	H	W
E	J	S	A	F	E	O	E

Story

1 **Read. Find two examples from the story.**

1 Helen always thinks about her family.

> [4] "but can I really leave the family right now?"
>
> [9] ....

2 It wasn't easy for Bob to look after the family.

> [8] ....
>
> [12] ....

3 The Supers help the Incredibles.

> [18] ....
>
> [19] ....

2 **Look at the picture. What can Elastigirl see, hear, and smell? How does she feel?**

She sees ....
She hears ....
She smells ....
She feels ....

3 [7] **Imagine you are on the train in New Urbem. Text a friend to tell them what is happening.**

Strange! The train .... the wrong way!

I'm ....! The train's going to ....!

Wait! Elastigirl ....
She ....

Phew! That was ....!

Are you OK?

Can you call for help?

Language

1 🎧 **Listen and read.**

> ### 💬 Language
>
> It stopped sudden**ly**. They smiled happ**ily**.
>
> Use an adverb (adjective + **-ly**) to say *how* something happens.
>
> We tried **hard**.   We played **well**.
>
> Some adverbs are irregular: **hard**, **fast**, **late**, **early**, **well**.

2 **Write. Change the underlined adjectives into adverbs.**

1 Her answers were <u>intelligent</u>. She answered ....

2 It was <u>hard</u> work. They worked ....

3 I was <u>angry</u> with my brother. I looked at my brother ....

4 It was an <u>early</u> dinner. They had dinner ....

5 He was a <u>dangerous</u> driver. He drove ....

6 She is a <u>good</u> painter. She paints ....

3 **Play a game. Mime and guess an activity. Use adverbs.**

You're driving fast!

That's right!

Verbs

play fight drive run
work jump sing
laugh dance walk

Adjectives

nice bad angry hard
careful brave slow
unhappy noisy fast

Phonics

1 🎧 Listen and circle.

1 str / st   aight

2 sc / scr   atch

3 str / st   and

4 str / st   ing

5 sk / scr   ate

6 sc / scr   eam

2 🎧 Write scr or str. Then listen and say.

Elastigirl ....etches and saves the train.

The city ....eets are safe again.

A ....ange message is on the ....een.

Who's the ....eenslaver and what does it mean?

De........oy the Supers—that's Evelyn's plan.

Who can help? The Incredibles can!

3 🎧 Listen and write the words. Then match the words with the same beginning sounds.

....

....

Values: Teamwork

1 How did these Supers help save the city? Think and say.

Mr. Incredible

Violet and Dash

Voyd

Frozone

2 Do the quiz. Are you a team player? Count your score.

Write a number: 3 = very true   2 = sometimes true   1 = not true

1 I listen to my teammates' ideas. ◯

2 I help my team with their work. ◯

3 I work hard for the team. ◯

4 I like sharing my ideas with the team. ◯

5 All the people in my team are important. ◯

Results:

11–15 = Nice job! You're a great team player.
6–10 = Okay. Now try harder.
1–5 = You have a lot to learn about teamwork. Start now!

3 Share.

> I gave three points to question 1. I always listen to my teammates. Then we choose the best idea.

4 Read and talk. How can you work as a team?

Imagine you and your friends want to raise money for a charity. What can you do? Talk and choose the best idea. Decide who does what.

Find Out

1 What are the differences between the two types of car? Write notes.

> **driverless cars**
>
> ....
>
> ....
>
> ....

> **regular cars**
>
> ....
>
> ....
>
> ....

2 What do the two types of car have in common?

Writing tip

What **is a driverless car?**

> Use a question word to ask for specific information.

3 Write the questions.

1 ....

<u>A computer</u> drives a driverless car.

2 ....

The sensors are <u>at the front, back, and sides of the car</u>.

3 ....

Driverless cars are good for older people <u>because they can't or don't want to drive</u>.

4 ....

They first thought about driverless cars <u>a hundred years ago</u>.

Game Connect Four in a Line

1 Say it.

Screenslaver .... from the building. Elastigirl .... him in her ....

2 Complete using adverbs.

I walk ....
You walk ....

3 Spell it.

I can see a s........ ....aight ....eet on my ....een.

4 True or False?

Bob is working hard at home.

5 Make two sentences. Use these words.

1 message screen
2 safe city

6 What can you do in a driverless car?

7 What happens first?

catch

chase

8 Who says this? Why?

"You're not good. You're Super."

9 Who drives a driverless car?

?

10 Match the opposites.

safe   illegal
allowed   in danger
hypnotize   wake up

11 Choose the odd one out.

destroy

control

crash   kill

12 Make a sentence. Use an adverb.

13 Spell it.

I .... eam when I am ....ared!

14 Show it.

I dance well.

I sing badly.

15 Say it.

At the beginning of the story, Supers were .... At the end, they were ....

16 Who is a team player?

Bill: When I have a good idea, I don't tell my classmates!

Jake: When I have a good idea, I share it with others.

Now I can ...

○ understand what happens and why in a story about a special family.

○ say how something happens using adverbs.

○ read, spell, and say words with str and scr.

49

1 🅰️ **Read and match 1–6 to a–f.**

1 A room in a house. ....

2 You put your trash in it. ....

3 You study there. ....

4 You move it to stop or start a thing. ....

5 A police officer. ....

6 A place for people who do bad things. ....

a sheriff

b college

c prison

d attic

e dumpster

f switch

2 📖 **Read and circle T (true) or F (false).**

1 Andy's mom took the bag outside because she thought it was trash. T / F

2 The toys wanted to go to Sunnyside because they didn't like Andy. T / F

3 Buzz put the toys in prison because he couldn't remember them. T / F

4 Lotso was angry with Daisy because she wasn't nice. T / F

5 Andy went to Bonnie because he wanted her to have his toys. T / F

3 💬 **Write. Use the words in brackets and *going to*.**

1 .... (what / you / do) on the weekend?

2 .... (I / visit) my aunt. How about you?

3 .... (we / go) to the park.

.... (we / eat) lunch.

Then .... (I / play) video games with Ben.

1 Ⓐⓐ **Look, read, and write.**

1 Moana is _____ing her boat.
The w_____ are big.

2 Moana is in a c_____.
She sees the t_____.

3 He's going to a_____ the
crab with his h_____.

4 Through the dar_____s,
Moana can see an i_____.

2 📖 **Read the questions. Write.**

1 What was the green stone? It was Te Fiti's _____.

2 Who attacked Moana and Maui's boat? Little _____.

3 What was Maui's power? He could change into different _____.

4 What gave Maui his power? The _____.

5 Who really was Te Kā, the fire monster? She was _____

_____.

3 💬 **Write. Use** *can* **or** *could*.

1 It often snows in our town, in winter. It _____ be really cold.

2 This chair doesn't look strong. It _____ break.

3 Please be quiet. Loud noises _____ scare the birds.

4 Cats love sleeping. They _____ sleep 15 hours a day!

1 🅰ⓐ **Read and match the words (a–f) to the definitions (1–6).**

a hyena
b stampede
c valley
d warthog
e jungle
f paw

1 A large number of animals running fast. ⋯⋯⋯

2 A thick forest in a hot place with many large plants. ⋯⋯⋯

3 An African animal that eats plants. ⋯⋯⋯

4 An African animal, like a dog, that eats meat. ⋯⋯⋯

5 An animal's foot. ⋯⋯⋯

6 The lower land between two mountains. ⋯⋯⋯

2 📖 **Read and check the main ideas in the story.**

◯ Do not believe all the things people tell you.

◯ Your family never lies to you.

◯ You can learn from the past, but you can't change it.

◯ Bad people always win.

3 💬 **Write. Use the past tense.**

1 ⋯⋯⋯⋯⋯⋯⋯⋯⋯⋯⋯⋯⋯⋯⋯⋯ (what/you/do) yesterday?

2 ⋯⋯⋯⋯⋯⋯⋯⋯⋯ (I/go) shopping with my dad. ⋯⋯⋯⋯⋯⋯⋯⋯
(we/buy) books and toys. ⋯⋯⋯⋯⋯⋯⋯ (we/eat) ice cream at *Ices*.

3 ⋯⋯⋯⋯⋯⋯⋯⋯⋯⋯⋯⋯ (you/have) their chocolate ice cream?

4 Yes, ⋯⋯⋯⋯⋯⋯⋯⋯. But ⋯⋯⋯⋯⋯⋯⋯⋯ (I/not like) it.

1 🄰🄰 **Choose and write.**

> sword   mend   competition   brave   spell   free

1 _____ people aren't afraid.

2 A witch's _____ can change a person into an animal.

3 You can cut things with a _____.

4 The best sports person wins the _____.

5 You can do what you like. You are _____.

6 The clock doesn't work. Can you _____ it?

2 📖 **Look and answer the questions.**

1 Where is Merida?
She's at the _____.

2 Why is she there?
She wants a _____.
She _____ her mother.

3 What is the witch doing?
She's making a _____.

3 💬 **Write. Use _to_ + verb or verb + _ing_.**

1 They enjoy _____ (watch) sports on TV.

2 He hates _____ (listen) to this kind of music.

3 We finished _____ (clean) the house at noon.

4 Do you want _____ (play) soccer?

5 They started _____ (run) because they were late.

6 I'm learning _____ (speak) Spanish.

1 **Aa** **Choose the correct answer: a, b or c.**

1 He couldn't .... the car because there was ice on the road, so it crashed.

    a control   **b** plan   **c** start

2 My friend and I worked .... and we finished very quickly.

    a best   **b** together   **c** nearly

3 Joy and sadness are ....

    a memories   **b** powers   **c** emotions

4 There was .... in our family because we couldn't find my baby brother!

    a hope   **b** panic   **c** disgust

5 Dad got .... with us because we broke the TV.

    a unhappy   **b** worst   **c** mad

2 **Read and write. Use one word.**

All **1** .... are important: you can't have joy without **2** .... It is **3** ....
to show your emotions. Talk about how you **4** .... with your friends and family.

3 **Write. Use superlative adjectives.**

1 This is .... (big) box we have.

2 Manuel is .... (good) player on the team.

3 This is .... (important) thing to remember.

4 What is .... (easy) way to do this?

5 This is .... (bad) memory I have.

6 Elena is .... (intelligent) person I know.

1 **Aa** **Write one word. Keep the meaning the same.**

1 You are not in danger.
You are _____ .

2 He drove quickly through
the city.
He _____ through
the city.

3 I wrote a text on my phone and
sent it to you.
I sent you a _____ .

4 You can't do this. It is not
allowed!
You can't do this. It is
_____ !

5 I followed the thief and tried to
catch him.
I _____ the thief.

6 Sam hit Joey and Joey hit Sam.
Sam and Joey _____ .

2 **Answer the questions. Write the names (Evelyn, Helen, or Bob). Then match the examples (a–c) to the answers.**

1 Who doesn't like the Supers? _____ ◯

2 Who thinks about the family? _____ ◯

3 Who is having a difficult time? _____ ◯

a Bob was at home with the kids. He felt tired.

b "But can I really leave the family right now?"
said Helen.

c "Supers are never going to be legal," Evelyn laughed.

3 **Write. Change the adjectives into adverbs.**

1 He is always nice and speaks very _____ .   polite

2 She's the best because she works _____ .   hard

3 We must leave very _____ tomorrow.   early

4 I couldn't catch her. She ran very _____ .   fast

5 They can swim very _____ .   good

Reading Record

Book 1
Toy Story 3

My rating: ☆☆☆☆☆

This book:

My new words:

STAMP

Book 2
Moana

My rating: ☆☆☆☆☆

This book:

My new words:

STAMP

Book 3
The Lion King

My rating: ☆☆☆☆☆

This book:

My new words:

STAMP

Book 4
Brave

My rating: ☆☆☆☆☆

This book:

My new words:

STAMP

Book 5
Inside Out

My rating: ☆☆☆☆☆

This book:

My new words:

STAMP

Book 6
The Incredibles 2

My rating: ☆☆☆☆☆

This book:

My new words:

STAMP

Spelling Practice

Common words	Look and write.	Cover and write.		✔
didn't				
could				
must				
mustn't				
about				
between				
than				
before				
after				
really				
together				
without				
most				
hundred				
thousand				
tonight				
weekend				
morning				
afternoon				
evening				
Monday				
Tuesday				
Wednesday				
Thursday				
Friday				
Saturday				
Sunday				

Superlative adjectives	Look. Write the second word.	Cover and write.		✔
good → best				
bad → worst				
kind → kindest				
smart → smartest				
sad → saddest				
happy → happiest				
Adverbs of manner				
good → well				
hard → hard				
fast → fast				
late → late				
early → early				
quick → quickly				
slow → slowly				
careful → carefully				
angry → angrily				
Irregular past tense verbs				
do → did				
have → had				
go → went				
say → said				
see → saw				
get → got				
eat → ate				
drink → drank				
sleep → slept				
run → ran				

Word List

a

a piece of
afraid
after
ago
amygdala
angrily
apart
appear
archery
attack
attic

b

back
back
bake
basket
battle
beach
bear
become
before
best
blue
bone
bow
box

brain
brave
break
breathe
bridge
build

c

cake
camera
carry
catch
cave
character
chase
choose
chute
classroom
cloth
college
come on
competition
control
core
could
cowgirl
crab

crash
cried
cub
cut

d

danger
dangerous
dangerously
darkness
day
daycare center
dead
deep
describe
desert
destroy
die
disgusted
dolphin
driverless
drop
drum
dumpster

e

east
eat
emotion

engineer
erupt

f

field
fight
film-maker
fire
fix
flashlight
flew
fly
food
free
front
frontal lobe
future

g

glue
going to
green
ground
group

h

happy
happily
hard
heart

60

helicopter
hello
hide
history
hockey
home
hook
hop
hope
hour
how
hunt
hurt
hyena
hypnotize

illegal
information
intelligent
intelligently
island

jungle

keep
kill
king

kingdom
kite

lake
land
large
lava
legal
liar
lie
light
lion
lioness
little
lovely

mad
mall
marry
meerkat
memory
mend
message
million
mind
model
monster

moon
more
most
must

nearly
negative
new
night
nose

paint
panic
parachute
part
past
paw
perfect
pie
pink
pirate
plan
plane
police officer
possible
power
practice

pretend
prison
protect
pull
purple
push

race
raincoat
real
really
reef
rice
rock
rocket
roof

safari
safe
sail
save
say
scratch
scream
screen
secret
sensor

sheriff

ship

size

sketch

sky

sleep

smell

smile

so

sound

space ranger

spell

spoon

stampede

star

start

statue

stew

stitch

stone

straight

strange

street

stretch

string

strong

suddenly

surprise

switch

sword

tapestry

taste

teach

test

thread

tissue

together

tracker

trash

treasure

true

trust

truth

tube

turn

unhappy

valley

voice

volcano

warthog

watch

wave

wheel

when

where

who

why

wildebeest

win

wind

window

witch

without

wonderful

worried

worst

yellow